FIFTY & Fabulous

Presented by

Dr. Sharon H. Porter

Copyright © 2019 Perfect Time SHP LLC

All rights reserved. This book is protected under the copyright laws of the United States of America.

No portion of this book may be reproduced, stored in a retrieval system, or transmitted in any form including photocopying, recording, or other electronic or mechanical methods, without the prior written permission of the publisher, except in the case of brief quotations embodied in reviews and certain other non-commercial uses permitted by copyright law.

Published by Write the Book Now, an imprint of Perfect Time SHP LLC.

Ordering Information:

For information regarding special discounts on bulk purchases, please contact the publisher: Perfect Time SHP LLC Publishing info@perfecttimeshp.com.

www.perfecttimesheppublishing.com

DEDICATION

This book is dedicated to all the amazing women who have been blessed to see their 50th birthday and beyond. If only we knew then what we know now...Even still, we are living our best life.

Fifty is amazing

TABLE OF CONTENTS

1 My 50 Sense - Kara D. Freeman 1

2 My Year of 50 - Linette Michelle Howard 17

3 Fifty, Fabolous, and Faithfilled - Nikki Williams Miller 29

4 My Grace Year - Sonya Powers Waddell 45

5 How I Slayed Her - Towanda R. Livingston 51

6 Journey to 50 - Martha Cooper-Hudson 65

7 Phenomenally 50 - Dr. Sharon H. Porter 75

Kara D. Freeman

Kara D. Freeman is Vice President of Administration and Chief Information Officer (CIO) of a Washington, DC based higher education association. With more than 30 years of experience, Freeman is recognized as a leader in the information technology field by the non-profit IT community, receiving several industry awards for her work.

Freeman holds a B.S. from the University of Maryland, Baltimore County and an M.B.A. from The George Washington University (DC), both in management information systems. She also holds a project management professional credential through the Project Management Institute and a certified association executive (CAE) credential through the American Society of Association Executives (ASAE).

Freeman is an avid college basketball fan and, as a season ticket holder, enjoys attending basketball games of the Georgetown University's men's basketball team in her spare time.

She is a native of Washington, DC and currently resides in Davidsonville, MD.

My 50 Sense

Kara D. Freeman

Wow...the year of my 50th birthday. I remember thinking 50 years old meant that you were just that..."old." I now know that turning 50 means you have lived long enough to learn from mistakes and, with that accumulated wisdom, live life to its fullest.

Always pensive on my birthday, turning 50 years old made me realize more years are likely behind me than in front of me. Celebrating this milestone birthday, I paused and considered: *What have I accomplished? What is my legacy?*

I have accomplished quite a bit, surprising even myself at times. My life has had many trials, missteps, and failures as well. Through the tough times is where some of my greatest lessons were learned.

Today, as a 50 year old African-American recently divorced woman living life on her own terms, I believe I have a thing or two to share about life.

Life has not always been easy but backing down from a challenge has never been my style. I'm hopeful that sharing some of the highlights and lowlights of my journey will make someone else's journey easier. My legacy can then be in helping someone else reach their life's goals.

When there is shine, there is always a corresponding grind. From the outside looking in, my life might look like a fairytale. The social media posts of galas, trips to sporting events, vacations abroad, and fun family times can be misleading. There is no doubt that life is great and parts do feel like a fairytale. However, there has been a serious 30 year grind that not everyone has witnessed. My work ethic is matched by few and has caused me to miss family moments and important life events. My demanding jobs have also been the cause of lost relationships over the years. But, as you will read, I have learned from these past mistakes.

Excellence is the best deterrent to racism or sexism. I heard Oprah Winfrey say this years ago and she is correct. Working in the IT industry since 1989, at times as the only woman, youngest executive, and only person of color at the table or in the entire company (yes, that happened!), I have had to deal with sexual harassment, racism, sexism, and ageism. Pretty much any –ism you can imagine has been a hurdle. Through all of it, I operated in excellence. My work has always been stellar. Never give someone the power to make you lower your own standards. That power is what they want. No matter the hurdle, operating in excellence cannot be denied and you remain in control.

To excel in diverse environments requires understanding and appreciation of more than just your own culture. My family moved from Southwest, Washington, DC to Prince George's County, Maryland when I was a young child. We were the first African-American family on our neighborhood street. Even though we lived in Maryland, we still attended the same predominantly African-American Catholic church and school in Southeast D.C. along with a large number of our extended family members. Growing up in a predominantly White neighborhood while attending a predominantly African-American church and school gave me a very strong appreciation of my own culture and an understanding of the culture of others. While our neighborhood quickly became predominantly African-American and we later transferred to public school in Maryland, the lessons learned from living and growing up with friends of many different cultures and backgrounds served me well and set my foundation of being able to thrive in diverse environments.

A can-do attitude sets the stage for success. My mother was the single most influential person in my life. She was a very kind person who had the tenacity to set goals and hit them. From her comes my never-say-never attitude. An early memory I have is attempting to tie my shoe and crying to my mother "I can't do it." Her reply was "Take the word 'can't' out of your vocabulary." She would repeat this mantra to me and my siblings many times over the years. It really did set us up for success in life. To this day, I have absolutely no doubt that I can do anything.

Outside of your comfort zone is where the magic happens. At 17 years old, I proclaimed "I have gone to school for 12 years. I know everything. What else could I possibly have to learn?" After she rolled her eyes upward and shook her head, my mother told me that I was indeed heading to college. She'd found the 3 grocery bags of college offers hidden in my closet, received after I scored very high on standardized tests. I thank God for her wisdom in understanding how to push her daughter outside my comfort zone. Attending college changed the trajectory of my life socially, culturally, intellectually, and financially.

Just be on time and show up everyday. These are the words my father said to me when I got my first job. A man who is not afraid of hard work, my dad told me that most people are late and do not go to work every day. According to my dad: "If you are on time and show up everyday, you'll be ahead of 80% of the people." There was no actual data or survey to support his statement but, over the years, I have found his words to be true. A strong work ethic has been a huge differentiator over the course of my career.

Life goes on after you lose a loved one. My parents were married for 50 years when my mother passed away in 2012. I thought the breath would leave my very body when my mom, my rock, died from pancreatic cancer. She was my biggest cheerleader and the one who had always pushed me to do more. One of my mother's sayings was "Life goes on" after we lost someone close to us. This would always get me upset because it seemed so insensitive. Now, I know she was absolutely correct. It may take some time to get your legs underneath you but life does and must go on after you lose a loved one.

A God-centered home with high expectations and love sets a strong foundation. Growing up, we did not have a lot of money but we had a lot of love. Both of my parents regularly told us "I love you" and showed it. They made sure we knew that our faith in God is what guides and keeps us.

They also made known their expectations that we would not get in trouble, stay on the right track, and work towards various goals. We had the added incentive of my father being a strong disciplinarian. Today, my three sisters, brother, and I are very close to one another and say "I love you" without hesitation. Because of the way we grew up, all five of us love and support one another unconditionally. Having this safety net and knowing I always have a place to go if something goes terribly wrong has allowed me to live my life without fear of failure.

Gaining career work experience while in college puts you ahead of the pack. I attended college as an undergraduate at the University of Maryland Baltimore County (UMBC) and, beginning my junior year, participated in the Cooperative Education (Co-op) Program which places students in jobs in their chosen career field. As an information systems management major, I worked for two IT corporations as a co-op student. While this added a year to my graduation date, it also put me ahead of the game when the time came to find a job because I had relevant work experience with leading companies in the industry.

Take advantage of great opportunities, even if it means working a little (or a lot) harder. After graduating from

UMBC, I began working as a systems analyst in the telecommunications industry. My employer had a program where they would pay 100% of the tuition towards your master's degree as long as it was in a job-related field. It was extremely difficult and quite tiring to work full-time and attend graduate school in the evenings at The George Washington University for three full years. However, I pushed through and was rewarded by graduating with an MBA and no associated debt.

Your reputation will precede you. On my job, my work ethic and leadership skills were noticed early and I very quickly moved into management and up the ranks to lead IT development teams for several telecommunications companies. Each promotion and new job came as the result of someone who knew my reputation as a leader with excellent skills and a strong work ethic reaching out to me to make me an offer.

Always operate in excellence and integrity. You never know who is watching. It was my reputation as a leader who operates in excellence, my brand, that landed me a job with a telecommunications start-up company. I was recommended for the job by my manager who I actually thought did not like me because I always (professionally) let him know when I disagreed with him. It turns out, he respected my candor when I addressed issues with him. He recommended me for the game-changing job of my career, building an IT organization from the ground up.

Sometimes the reward from hard work does not happen immediately. My work at the startup company was the toughest job I have ever had. I built the entire IT team and infrastructure, including implementing all of the technology systems used inside the company. We worked 14-16 hour days, seven days a week to get that company off the ground. We were motivated by the excellent salary and potential for a multi-million dollar reward when the company went public, or so we thought. I eventually became very ill from working at that pace for almost two years and was advised by my doctor to leave my job "or die." The reality of her words hit hard. The company did not go public after all and it seemed that I'd wasted two years of my life. The reward for this work would come years later.

There is something to learn from and in every situation. The startup company did not go public and we did not become rich. A lot was learned, though, about running a business, initial public offerings (IPOs) and investing in stock. After participating in the IPO of a partner company, I made a significant financial gain. This financial gain allowed me to later take a hiatus from working at all, a decision I would come to regret.

Always have a goal, beginning with the end in mind. I later worked for several other start-up companies, one of which was located in the United Kingdom (UK), allowing me to travel to London every six weeks to the home location. From startups, I learned a lot about how to lead a team and successfully or unsuccessfully run an organization. During this time, with no real plan for my life, I made a lot of money and squandered a lot of money too. My only goal was to make money so once I did that, I made several questionable decisions which put me at risk of starting over.

Remain humble and never be ashamed to ask for help. I planned to take six months off from working and live off money from my investments. Well, six months quickly turned to nine months and then to one year and still there was no job. Try as I might, I could not find a job in the IT field. I humbled myself, accepted an administrative assistant position with a temporary agency, and considered moving in with a family member. Hitting this low point and no longer the "big IT executive", I reached out to close friends and let them know what was happening. One of my friends recommended me for a mid-level job with a large corporation, working in my career field. I was back in business and, again, quickly moved up in management due to my strong work ethic and now-broadened skills gained from working with start-up companies. This situation taught me to not let my job define my worth and to never be too proud to ask for help.

There is much more to life than career. My work ethic has been a double-edged sword. It has catapulted my career and it has also caused major issues. At times, my health has been at risk and I gained a lot of weight because work was the only priority and exercise was not important. I also lost relationships due to the 24x7 nature of my job. I remember leaving a date because I was paged by my job. He let me know that he no longer wanted a relationship with a woman whose job was more important than him. At the time, I thought he was ridiculous and self-absorbed. I now realize there was truth in what he said. My job had become my life. So, I gained a lot career-wise but I missed out on life events, like marriage and kids. Thankfully, life balance, with health as a priority and my own family, would come later.

Find work you love and believe in. I eventually found my calling in the nonprofit industry, still working in the IT field.

Working for an organization whose mission you believe in makes the tough days a lot easier to manage. Initially, my role was much smaller at the non-profit organization. However, again my work ethic and skills were noticed and I became the head of the IT department. Promotion into the Vice President and Chief Information Officer (CIO) role would follow. I was eventually asked to take on responsibility for additional areas of the organization and the role of Vice President, Administration and CIO which I have been for 10 years now.

Joy in our sisterhood. In 1994, I was initiated into the illustrious sisterhood of Delta Sigma Theta Sorority, Inc. It is difficult to put into words how being a member of this sisterhood of civic and community-oriented, college educated women has positively impacted my life. I have a loving support system like no other and am afforded many opportunities to help my community as well. Delta Sigma Theta Sorority, Inc. has been a true blessing to me and I am eternally grateful to be a member of this wonderful organization.

Your circle of friends impacts your trajectory, positively or negatively. My very small circle of friends, both male and female, plays a major role in my life. My good friends support me and hold me accountable and I do the same for them. They do not always agree and will tell me, with love, when I am wrong. The bottom line is we trust, respect, and learn from one another, sharing insights on jobs, career, and family.

A lot can be learned from being quiet and listening. A lot of people at my job were either buying homes or talking about it. Wanting to participate in the discussions, I purchased my first home at 23 years old. Twenty years later, noticing that several coworkers headed across the Chesapeake Bay Bridge to their beach homes on the weekends, I did some financial analysis and purchased a beach home as an investment. When you really listen to the conversation, not necessarily trying to contribute, you can learn a lot.

Excellent credit reduces stress and enables financial freedom. I spent my 20's messing up my credit buying things I did not need and paying bills late. I then spent my 30's repairing my credit. Already owning a home helped a lot. Taking time to understand how credit scores are calculated and learning to operate within those guidelines increased my very low credit score to an "excellent" credit rating within a few years. Having great credit removed so much stress from my life. Financial literacy should really be taught in middle and high school.

There is joy in helping others. What has sustained me over the years is telling my story and motivating others to help them reach their goals. A positive impact is made by mentoring others, advocating for them, or seeing their potential and promoting them into positions which stretch them to grow even further. When you have been blessed, there is a responsibility to pass along to others what you have learned.

Balance in life is important. I was in my mid-forties when I was married and became a mother to my husband's two children. Becoming a wife and mother changed my priorities immediately and I loved it. Instead of my evenings being filled with work, they were filled with cooking dinner, assisting with homework, attending the boys' baseball practices, and working out with my husband. While my marriage did not last the way my parents' marriage did, I gained so much from it. I learned how to put my job in its right place in my life and find balance, to include exercise and self-care. So, marriage and motherhood blessed me immensely.

Turning 50 years old brought with it wisdom and a clarity of purpose. I have learned that the lessons are in the journey and the joy is in the moments. In the moments are where you find love, happiness, trust, and friendship.

Weathering my ups and downs, with God at the center of my life, I stand proud as a financially stable C-suite executive who has a loving heart, strong desire to help others, and a great circle of supportive family, sorors, and friends. I am abundantly blessed, enjoying myself, and living life the way I want, with no excuses.

And that, my friends, is my 50 sense!

Linette Michelle Howard

Linette Michelle Howard was born and raised in what used to be called "The Chocolate City" as well as in the 1990's the city that was named the "Murder Capital", Washington D.C. This truly shaped and made her into the strong, black, beautiful, Fifty&Fabulous woman that she is today. She wouldn't change a thing!

As a wife and a mother figure to her nephew and a freelance Christian makeup artist, she is challenged daily on trying to find ways to maneuver it all, and still succeed in her mind, in her health and in her business and also accomplish the plans that God has created for her, in connection with her newly created ministry. Although at times it is a little overwhelming, her philosophy is "If it doesn't challenge you, then it won't change you".

My Year of 50

LINETTE MICHELLE HOWARD

Let me first just bow my head and lift my hands in total honor and total praise to our Almighty God, for having allowed me to reach my 50th year in life so polished, passionate and poised by his incredible and Amazing Grace. It is all because of God that I am still here and I am exceedingly and immensely thankful for all that he has done for me and still continues to do. I am also truly thankful to Dr. Sharon Hargro Porter the Visionary for this 50 & Fabulous collaboration and all of the other 50 & Fabulous women who are a part of this Anthology, 1969 was a GREAT YEAR, because some Stars were born!

My Road to 50....

It is an absolute blessing for me to have made it through all that I have been through and still be so full of life and absolute pure joy. I am still pinching myself in amazement of how different I am , how much stronger I am, how much wiser I am, and how beautifully and wonderfully made I am to myself right now. You see, I haven't always seen the wonderfully or the beautifully made when I looked in my mirror. All I saw was all of the mean and ugly words and labels that people had loaded me down with all of my life. But today, as I stand here in full majesty and full grandeur of myself, 50 & Sooo Fabulous I vow to you and to God that from this day forth that all I'll see is what God sees in me and all that I am is what God says that I am, Fearfully and Wonderfully made and Wonderful are his works!

Fifty is nothing like I envisioned it to be when I was 25 years old. Thank God for that, otherwise I'd be an old lady at the end of my life, with no more mountains to climb and no more risks to take, but luckily for me, that as far as I know, I am not even close to being at the end of my life, Praise be to God.

The greatest chapter of my life, has only just begun…. My year of 50!

Self-Love, It really is the most Greatest Love of All.
So as far as I can remember I've always loved myself right, or so I thought anyway, because I had always protected myself, adorned myself with the latest fashions and kept myself well groomed, so yeah one would speculate that I did in fact love

myself right. That was until I found myself pregnant at the age of 23 and living with my baby's daddy in his grandmother's house. After five months of my pregnancy my ex-boyfriend called and told me that my current boyfriend cheated on me and gotten someone else pregnant. He had another girl pregnant and she was further along than I was, seven months to be exact. Needless to say, I went into an immediate state of depression and I cried every single day, I subsequently lost the baby which only deepened my depression, it was then that I began to sit in the chair beside his grandmother's bed and glean from her wisdom and the one thing that she would always say to me was **"you have to love yourself"**. She'd always preach to me every day or as often as she could, how important it was for me to love myself. But I did love myself right? Didn't you just hear me say that I wore the latest fashions, I got my hair and nails done, I brushed my teeth and I had a bomb hair weave back then, so duh yes I loved myself, who doesn't love themselves? It's an innate feeling or emotion that you are born with, so it's almost like you are duly obligated to love yourself, it's a requirement for life!

But I didn't get it back then and I could never understand why she was telling this young beautiful woman, who clearly loved herself the same thing every day, **"you have to love yourself"**....

Needless to say, that I would go through the next 27 years of my life not really knowing or realizing what Vivian Taylor was really saying when she would tell me that I have to love myself, until just recently when I joined this book collaboration made of 50 & Fabulous women and I needed to decide what I would write about, so I searched through the memories of my life and because this particular event made such a huge impact on my young adult life, I started reliving it all over again, so much so that I can still hear (Mother) saying, **"you have to love yourself"**... And then all of a sudden something just clicked in my head, what she was really saying is that, how can you think or say that you love yourself when you are dating this boy, who lives with his grandmother and who has cheated on you with another girl and now has that same girl pregnant with a baby on the way and as a result of that pregnancy and betrayal. You've now miscarried your own baby and now you are in a full state of depression! Now how can you say that you love yourself in all of this mess, where is the self-love in that?....

Fully aware now that there is no way humanly possible that I could have even remotely have loved myself the way that a strong, black and intelligent woman should love herself or at least half as much as I loved this boy, (and that still would've been a lot) and although she was trying to say it in the nicest way possible without calling me an idiot, because that is truly not what I needed at the time, she found favor with me and she tried to reach the little girl inside of me who had never really had anyone to say to her **"you have to love yourself"** and to not let anyone mistreat you, because you have so much value inside of you, more value than you'll ever know.

50 Life Lessons

1. Pray & Trust God.
2. Lean not unto your own under-standing and in all your ways acknowledge God and he will direct your path.
3. **LOVE YOURSELF.**
4. Forgive.
5. Believe half of what you see and none of what you hear.
6. Pray & Trust God.
7. Always be honest with yourself and with others.
8. Be yourself.
9. Show up for your life every single day.
10. Pray & Trust God.
11. Be FABULOUS!
12. Never hold onto anything tighter than you hold on to God!
13. Be content and grateful for what you have and just keep going!

14. Don't compare yourself to anyone else!
15. You are just as DOPE as them!
16. Pray & Trust God.
17. You always have more than you think you have
18. Be fearless.
19. Don't worry about what your haters say, they're STUPID!
20. Only tell people what you want them to know.
21. Pray & Trust God.
22. Don't be a follower.
23. When you are wrong, say you're sorry, it really takes a load off and it makes you better!
24. Love your Family & Friends.
25. Whatever you are thinking about doing somebody else is already doing, so do it now!!
26. Trust God's plan for your life.
27. Your life has a purpose, so ask God what it is.
28. Enjoy every second of your life because before you know it'll all be over!
29. Laugh every single day!
30. Let no man or woman bring you so low as to hate him or her. MLK
31. Pray & Trust God.
32. Not everyone that smiles at you is your friend!
33. Say THANK YOU!

34. Schedule me time for yourself.
35. Get a spiritual mentor.
36. Pray & Trust God.
37. Don't be afraid to be different.
38. Don't wait for people to encourage you, encourage yourself!
39. Don't chase people!
40. Exercise and drink a lot of water!
41. Everyone has power, so know and own your power!
42. **LOVE YOURSELF!!**
43. Pray & Trust God.
44. Protect your peace.
45. Keep a journal of life's events so when it comes time for you to write a book, you're ready!
46. Believe in yourself.
47. Don't waste nine years of your life at a job that you hate!
48. Crying is therapeutic, so don't be too proud and strong to do it, you need to do it, it will make you stronger!
49. Pray & Trust God.
50. Trials and tribulations come to make you stronger and to move you into the divine purpose that God has ordained for your life, it's not punishment, it's your destiny!

And finally I can't stress this enough, the importance of loving yourself. Loving yourself is more than merely just brushing your teeth, getting your nails done or wearing the latest or hottest fashion trends, that does not charter self-love (so nope! wearing Gucci and Christian Louboutin's is not self-love) that is only cosmetic treatment for the outer parts of your body, and oftentimes in grooming those parts of yourself, you give yourself and others the false sense of reassurance that you do in fact love yourself, when in reality you are simply pretending to love yourself, because in reality you don't quite know how to love yourself, or it could be that perhaps no one has ever told you that loving yourself is a prerequisite for any other love that follows.

Self-love is the root of all love and at the very core of your being you are love and without love for yourself, you will be completely lost, looking for love in all the wrong places, people and things. Trying to fill a hole and void that only God and self-love can truly fill. Accept who you are (your strengths and your weaknesses), value who you are (you are a Queen), respect who you are (or nobody else will respect you) and appreciate who you are. The more you love yourself, the more you'll bring more love into your life. You are what you think you are and you are Love…

So Love Yourself, Celebrate Yourself, Encourage Yourself, Standup for Yourself, Cheer for Yourself, Spoil Yourself, Go Out On A Date with YOURSELF!!

Last year when I turned 49 years old or maybe even a little while before then, I started to feel like I wasn't doing enough in my Christian walk with God, and that after all he had done for me, this was the best that I could do? He had bestowed upon me, the will and the strength to live for 49 years and not bear resemblance to even half of what I had been through, and still be in my right mind and to be truly blessed to have a husband that simply adores and cares so much for me and this was the best that I could do? It was simply unacceptable for me and I wanted to do more, I needed to do more, so I went to him in prayer and asked if he would please tell me what more that I could do to prove to him that I loved him and that I was grateful and thankful to him, for all of those years that he had waited for me to realize that he loved me more than any man ever would, more than my mother and father ever would, more than any of my so called friends ever would and even more than I had the inept capacity to love myself. So as the months unfolded, the closer I got to 50, was the closer I walked with God and he started to (and still is) reveal what my true purpose was in life, and that is to worship and follow him. That was always my purpose and his plan for my life, but in order to get me to see and realize that, he had to take me through all of those dark and lonely places, and through all of those years that I would suffer through so much heartache and so much pain that, that I had completely and totally convinced myself that God hated me and never really loved me, just like none of those guys did that I had ever dated.

As I stand here right now, feeling fresh and brand new, I now realize that God loves me more than I'll ever even be able to comprehend and all of those guys and all of those broken friendships didn't last because they were not a part of God's eternal plan for my life, but still they all played an intricate part in my life's journey.

Thank you Father, for saving me and rescuing me from myself… and for loving me when I couldn't and didn't even know how to Love Myself.

I love you Father and for the rest of my life, I surrender my all and my will to you.

I now fully understand what Whitney Houston meant when she said, "Because the greatest Love of all, is happening to me. I found the greatest Love of all inside of me. The greatest love of all, is easy to achieve, learning to Love Yourself, It Is the Greatest Love of All…

My Year of 50 & Fabulous Begins NOW!

Nikki Williams Miller

Nikki is a native of Greenville, NC where she matriculated through Pitt County Schools. Upon graduating from J.H. Rose High School in 1987, she began her secondary studies at Spelman College in Atlanta, Georgia.

During her Junior year, she transferred to The University of North Carolina at Chapel Hill graduating with a Bachelor of Science Degree in 1991. After completing Elementary Education certification at East Carolina University, Nikki began her career as a 5th grade teacher in1994. In 2008, Nikki was accepted into the North Carolina Principal Fellows Program where she earned a Masters Degree in School

Administration in 2010. Nikki is licensed in North Carolina as a K-6 Elementary Teacher, a K-12 Principal and a Curriculum and Instructional Specialist.

Nikki has been a servant leader with Pitt County Schools as an Assistant Principal for the past 10 years. Nikki is a passionate Educator who strongly believes in developing authentic relationships with her students and teaching the whole child for academic and social success. She believes every child can learn and believes in equitable learning experiences for all children. She is a strong Educational Advocate for socioeconomically disadvantaged children. She works on purpose to ensure, especially for black and brown children, that they become successful high school graduates and enroll in colleges or universities, enlist in our armed services or enter the workforce, in an effort to decrease the classroom to prison pipeline statistics in our communities. She is a strong change agent in putting practices in place in schools to close the achievement gap amongst minority students, in particular, African American males.

Nikki became an Amazon #1 Best Selling Author in June 2018 with the release of the book *Dear Fear Volume 2* for which she was a Contributing Author. She is also a Collaborating Author *The Purposed Woman ~ A 365 Devotional* that was released on Amazon on April 23, 2019 and within 4 hours it became #1 in Christian Devotions, making Nikki a 2-time Amazon Best Selling Author. Nikki is very active in her church, Sycamore Hill Missionary Baptist Church where she has served as Praise and Worship Leader, Women's Ministries Chair, Sunday School Teacher, Youth Bible Study Teacher and as Co-Chair of the annual Women's Day Celebration.

Nikki is also a financial and active member of the Greenville (NC) Alumnae Chapter of Delta Sigma Theta Sorority, Inc. She currently serves as an Educational Advocate for North Carolina with Delta's National Educational Initiative T.A.G. ~ Teachers Advocating for Great Change under the Delta Research and Educational Foundation.

Having lost her mother unexpectedly on December 8, 2010 to complications following open heart surgery, she participates in the annual Down East Heart Walk, and she has annually promoted Go Red for Women Events through her church, sorority and school to raise awareness that Heart Disease is the #1 killer of women in America.

Nikki has been married to her husband Anthony Louis Miller for 27 years. To this union, they are blessed with two daughters, Gabrielle Nicole Miller, Esq. who works for the United States House of Representatives and Moriah Joelle a

Junior at North Carolina State University completing a Bachelor of Science Degree in Sport Management.

Nikki is the proud and blessed daughter of her Rock, her Dad, Raymond Wesley Williams. Nikki is also the doggie mom to a beautiful 3 year old Shih Tzu Macey Ann.

Nikki has resolved after 50 years of life, that only what you do for Christ will last and If I can help somebody, as I travel along. If I can help somebody, with a word or song. If I can help somebody, from doing wrong then my living shall not be in vain.

Fifty, Fabulous and Faithfilled
Nikki Williams Miller

On April 6, 2019 I celebrated 50 years of Life! This was one of the most exciting milestones of my 5 decades here on Earth. I intentionally began the year planning for this big day because I wanted to show women of all ages how to embrace this new season with great joy and anticipation of what Haggai 2:9 NKJV says, "The glory of this latter temple shall be greater than the former, says the Lord of hosts. And in this place I will give peace, says the Lord of hosts."

In the book of Leviticus 25* we find the 50th year called the Year of Jubilee. The word "Jubilee" literally, "ram's horn" in Hebrew, "Yobel" is defined in Leviticus 25:9 as the sabbatical year after seven cycles of seven years (49 years). The fiftieth year was to be a time of celebration and rejoicing for the Isaraelites. The ram's horn was blown on the tenth day of the seventh month to start the fiftieth year of the universal redemption. The year of Jubilee involved a year of release from indebtedness and all types of bondage. All prisoners and captives were set free, all slaves were released, all debts were forgiven, and all property was returned to its original owner. Thus, the 50th year is the year of Liberty!

Over the past 49 years, I have faced many lessons, tests, trials, challenges, tribulations and storms that have prepared me to be Fifty and Free! It is through these seasons that my Faith has been strengthened. Hebrews 11:1 "Now Faith is the substance of things hoped for, the evidence of things not seen." It is in this chapter that the writer of Hebrews, the Apostle Paul shares how many endured hardships that strengthened their Faith. It was Faith that allowed Abel to offer God an acceptable sacrifice that outshone that of Cain. Abel was declared righteous and approved by God because of this. Although Abel died, it was through his Faith that his voice was still heard. Enoch was taken up by the Lord and escaped the experience of death only because of his Faith, which was pleasing to God. The Faith of Abraham, Jacob and Isaac allowed them to follow the voice of God to an unknown place and inhabit a strange land for the promise of becoming heirs of righteousness. This same Faith allowed the elderly Abraham and his barren wife Sarah, to produce a son who eventually left them more descendents that could be counted. Moses risked the anger of the king and suffered abuse because of his Faith in a better life to come. This is how he was able to lead the people of God to freedom. There were women in biblical times who demonstrated extreme Faith in God's promise of better things to come. Mary, Eve, Naomi, Mary Magdalene, Tamar, Jehosheba, Lydia, Priscilla, Rahab, Esther, Ruth, Hannah, Deborah, and more were able to achieve great feats and attain just outcomes based on their Faith. Many faithful have endured imprisonment, chains, torture and even stoning and many other indignities, travesties, and even death. In the end, God commended their Faith and delivered on His promise of an afterlife that could not be perfect without the presence of the Faithful.

Throughout the history of America, there are countless examples of women who endured and became victorious because of their strong Faith. Harriet Beecher Stowe who was an author and abolitionist. Ameila Earhart, the first woman to fly solo across the Atlantic Ocean. After escaping slavery, Harriet Tubman turned her efforts into helping others break away into freedom. Sally Ride became the first woman in space in 1983. Best known for her refusal to give up her seat on the bus, Rosa Parks was a civil rights activist and played a pivotal role in the Montgomery bus boycott. Parks is known as the mother of the freedom movement. Oprah Winfrey, despite a lot of odds, became North America's first multibillionaire black woman and has been ranked as the top black philanthropist influencing the world through the power of media. Born into slavery, Sojourner Truth fought against racial inequalities in the 1850's. Susan B. Anthony played a pivotal role in the women's suffrage movement in our history in the 1870's. Madam C.J. Walker, as a single mother, was the first American woman to become a self-made millionaire through the hair-care empire that she built. Florence Nightingale trained and organized nurses to care for wounded soldiers during the Crimean War. Mother Teresa was awarded the Nobel Peace Prize in 1979 for her work in ministering to those others wouldn't even consider. Fanny Crosby, though totally blind, wrote more than 9,000 hymns that are most popular in churches across an array of denominations even today. Two of my favorite being, "Pass Me Not, O Gentle Savior" and "Blessed Assurance".

In Luke 17:6, the Lord says, "If you have Faith as a mustard seed, you can say to this mulberry tree, be pulled up by the roots and be planted in the sea, and it would obey you." It was not until I began my college journey at Spelman College as a freshman in 1987 that I can recollect the commencement of my Faith walk. Having grown up as a child attending Sunday School and Sunday Worship weekly at my local church, my spiritual foundation was built upon a solid rock.

Failure built Faith

As an only child, moving from Greenville, North Carolina to Atlanta, Georgia, nine hours away from all I had known for 17 years tested my Faith in God. Leaving behind my parents, my grandparents, my church family, other family and friends going to an unknown city and college, forced me to rely on all that was rooted in me spiritually to walk this unfamiliar path. Attending Spelman College was one of the richest experiences. It was at Spelman that I was introduced to the rich legacies of African American women. My Soror of Delta Sigma Theta Sorority, Inc. was inaugurated as the college's first African American woman president during the summer of my freshman year. I loved having to attend weekly Convocation in Sisters Chapel where we heard the voices of many influential women of our times. It was at Spelman that I learned failure academically. I became so involved with college activities and life in Atlanta that I did not balance my time well to ensure my success in class. I had a very hard course load my first semester that included chemistry and microbiology as I was initially majoring in Biology in pursuit of becoming a pediatrician. I **FAILED** my microbiology class and I was completely devastated. I was so afraid of how my parents would react to this failure. I had lived my formative years doing everything I could to please them and meet their expectations, and now I had to face disappointing them. I continued at Spelman but towards the end of my first semester sophomore year, I decided that I needed to change my plan. During one of our weekly Convocations, we had a Spelman Alumna visit us to speak who was a local dentist. When I heard her, my spirit leaped! I had spent summers during my high school years working with a local dentist who was the first African American Female to graduate from the Dental School at the University of North Carolina at Chapel Hill. During winter break I went to talk with her about my new plan to become a dentist. I applied to UNC's Dental Hygiene Program in January 1989 in hopes of attending their Dental School, I was accepted and transferred the beginning of my junior year and earned a Bachelor of Science degree in 1991. Just prior to my August 3, 1991 wedding, I sat for the North Carolina Dental Hygiene Licensing Exam and I **FAILED**. I found myself at a crossroad of great uncertainty about my career. I had devoted four years into a degree that I could not use at the time. This failure caused me to search my soul and determine which direction to go. I prayed and asked God to lead me and guide me. I was led to attend a church conference on *Spiritual Gifts* and at the end completed an assessment. Teaching was my greatest spiritual gift. I learned that our spiritual gifts are to edify the body of Christ, but they will also mirror your vocational gifts. I immediately applied to East Carolina University as a non degree graduate student and within two years completed certification for Elementary Education. The fear of failure gripped my soul because I had to take the North Carolina Teaching Licensure Exam. Remembering that I did not pass my Dental Hygiene exam, I found myself on bended knees praying to God to help me be successful. I passed with flying colors and began teaching 5th grade in 1994. Failure built my Faith!

Friends built Faith

Growing up as an only child, I craved building friendships at a very early age. My parents surrounded me with a village of amazing friends beginning as a toddler through birthday celebrations and other ocaissions. At the age of 9 years old, we moved into our new house into the neighborhood that was developed by my parents and some of their very close friends and my dad's fraternity brothers. The children in the neighborhood created a special bond that we have maintained through our adulthood. As I grew older, my friendship circle expanded to friends I made through church, school, and my extracurricular activities like dance. It was in my kindergarten class that a classmate who happened to be of a race and culture different from mine. She became my first best friend from day one! We enjoyed spending the night at each other's house, going on trips with our families and even attending so many other events together through Girl Scouts and our individual churches. Her family embraced me as their own and exposed me to sectors that I had not become familiar. We made a vow as little girls that we would remain best friends forever. After 50 years, that vow has not been broken. When I entered middle school and high school, my friendship circle widened even more. I enjoyed weekend slumber parties rotating at each other's house with a very special group of girlfriends, school events like sports and dances, participating in debutante programs through local sororities that our mothers were members, making lifetime memories. Most of my bridesmaids in my wedding were made up by friends that I held close from my primary and secondary schools, Spelman and UNC. After graduating from college and getting married, my friendship circle changed yet again. During this season of friendships, I learned the meaning of true friends through many tests. I experienced my greatest hurt from "friends" that attacked in so many ways from the age of 23 until 49 years old. I have always had certain expectations for friendships and I found out, the hard way, that others didn't hold the same value. These "friends" ended up not being trustworthy, didn't support me when I needed them, lied on me, verbally abused me, took advantage of my kindness, talked about me negatively to others, walked away from me with no explanation, never apologized when they were wrong, ended up not being loyal, were not dependable, weren't honest with me, always took from me and didn't reciprocate, didn't celebrate my successes or those of my children, didn't protect me being harmed in situations they could, and were unforgiving of my imperfections and mistakes. I invested a lot of money, time, energy and tears in certain friendships only to get painfully hurt. During the 6 months prior to my 50th birthday, I spent a 40 day period of time fasting and praying for God to lead and guide me to identify and discern who my real and genuine friends are in my life. I even sought professional counseling. I was determined that I was not going into my 50th year of life with the pain of dead friendships. My therapist helped me through the process of letting go of those relationships that were unhealthy. She recommended a list of self-help books and other resources during this time to help me find the answers. But the greatest book was my Bible. There I was reminded in Proverbs 18:24 "A man of many companions may come to ruin, but there is a friend who sticks closer than a brother." Proverbs 13:20 "He who walks with the wise grows wise, but a companion of fools suffers harms." John 15:13 "Greater love has no one than this, that he lay down his life for his friends." John 15:15 "No longer do I call you servants, for a servant does not know what his master is doing; but I have called you friends, for all things that I heard from My father I have made known to you." Friends built my Faith!

Fear Built Faith

On December 8, 2010 I had the most devastating day of my whole life. My mother was diagnosed through a heart catheterization with severe cardiovascular disease in November 2010 after she failed a stress test recommended by her primary care physician after experiencing shortness of breath for a period of time. While at home following her open heart bypass surgery, on the morning of December 8th, she stopped breathing. My mother, my sorority sister, very best friend, biggest cheerleader, confidant, best example of a phenomenal woman had a pulmonary embolism that took her away from us completely unexpectedly. For the first time in my life I wondered how in the world would I survive without my mother. Who would I go to when I needed advice? A good laugh? To confide something in without judgement? A shoulder to cry on? A mother's hug? I allowed fear to paralyze me. My mother saw her primary care physician yearly and I was just baffled at how no signs or symptoms led her to an earlier diagnosis of anything related to cardiovascular disease. After meeting with the cardiovascular surgeon who performed her open heart surgery, he helped me understand that this is the reason heart disease is called the "silent killer" and is the #1 killer of women in America. This knowledge suddenly forced me to not succumb to fear of my own health being impacted in a like manner, but rather become educated to help myself, my daughters, and other women have an awareness of living a heart healthy lifestyle. I began meeting with a health coach and my own primary care doctor who referred me to a cardiologist for screening. I started to become involved with the national American Heart Association's Go Red For Women Campaign by sharing it with my local chapter of Delta Sigma Theta Sorority, Inc. and together we began an annual event at local churches every February. I also participated in the annual Heart Walk in my area in memory of my mother. Again, I returned to God to ask Him to help me to ultimately overcome my fear. I was reminded of 2 Timothy 1:7 "For God has not given us a spirit of fear; but of power, and love, and of a sound mind." Fear built by Faith!

The beginning of Chapter 50 has been the absolute best year of my life! From the collective trials, tests and tribulations I have endured, it has truly made me a stronger woman in my Faith! I can confidently say that I am living the best season of my life with the expectation that the latter will be greater!

NIKKI WILLIAMS MILLER

Sonya Powers Waddell

Sonya Powers Waddell is the owner and operator of Simply Soul Restaurant and Catering and Simply Living Family Care Homes LLC, an assisted living community located in North Carolina. She is the mother of two beautiful children, Jimmie and Joi and grandmother to Brayden.

Sonya was born and raised in Winston-Salem, North Carolina. Her love for serving others directed her path into the restaurant/catering business as well as taking care of the elderly and handicap. Sonya's future aspirations include opening more assisted living homes.

You can connect with Sonya on Facebook at Simply Soul Restaurant.

MY GRACE YEAR
SONYA POWERS WADDELL

I call my 50th year my Grace year! This year I have experienced the Grace of God in my life in ways that I could have never expected! This year marks the end of a decade of grieving so many losses in my life.

The Losses...

The loss of my mom in 2010, after her courageous two-year battle with stage 4 lung cancer and to have to face the disgrace of my then ten year marriage be publicly destroyed 30 days to the date of my mom's passing was to say the ABSOLUTE least that my faith in God was put to the test like never before. While I felt at times that I was truly only EXISTING off the prayers of my children and the prayers that I had stored up from years of trusting that God only had a good plan for me! I trotted and trampled through the last decade wondering who had I become..... The last ten years I have doubted my faith, hated the God of my salvation, only to TRULY realize that it was HE who has NEVER LEFT ME NOR FORSAKEN ME!

My "Grace" YEAR...

The number five (5) represents Grace, and has always been one of my favorite numbers. As I reflect on the past 50 years of my entire life, I know that I know that it was GRACE that has brought me to this place of existing. Yes, I have had losses and as great as they were, I have also experienced *Great Grace* as well....

I have experienced, grace to survive my mom's passing realizing that she was given to me as an example of how to be a woman of virtue. I SAW her and now I AM her.... God graced me with the perfect mom who knew how to fight, love, support, give, and even bow-out gracefully all in due season! I see so much of my mom in me. We both worked in the healthcare industry, caring for the elderly. My mom had a catering business when I was younger. I would help her at all her events. I have always served in the hospitality and kitchen ministry at my church. I am server at heart. Look at me now, owner of a restaurant and a family care facility.

I have experienced, grace to survive divorce and yet know that I have never been forsaken or alone, even though I may have to walk alone in this life. I, along with my then husband, opened Simply Soul Restaurant and Catering in

Winston-Salem, NC in 2012. I have always wanted to open a restaurant. I have been running the restaurant alone since my divorce in 2016. It simply brings me joy.

As I sat alone in my home after my divorce, I wondered what would I do with this big house. My children were gone and I knew I didn't want to sell it. A friend reminded me that I had mentioned previously that I wanted to open a facility that cared for the elderly. I started researching and knew exactly what I would do with my home. I opened Simply Living Family Care Homes LLC, an assisted living community located in Rural Hall, NC. My passion to serve was inevitable.

I have experienced the grace of raising two of the most fearfully and wonderfully made gifts; my children, Jimmie & Joi Jeter. I only could have hoped for such gifts. Jimmie "JJ" Jeter, who is a renowned Broadway actor is currently performing in the Broadway production of Hamilton in New York City at the Rodgers Theater. My daughter, Joi has blessed me with the greatest gift of all, my first grandson, Brayden. Joi works right alongside me in each of my businesses. My children make me proud to be called a mom.

Thank you GOD my father, redeemer, supplier, and the lover of my entire soul for gracing my ENTIRE LIFE with your POWER! The best is yet to come!

Towanda R. Livingston

Towanda R. Livingston is a successful and award-winning Diversity and Inclusion Executive. She is an innovative thought equity, inclusion and supplier diversity leader of this era. Since beginning her professional career, Towanda has delivered transformational solutions for corporate and government agencies within the inclusion and supplier diversity space. Towanda has received numerous awards and industry accolades for developing, implementing and institutionalizing various diversity initiatives and programs for her work in communications, human capital management, and supplier/business and community outreach.

Towanda possesses over 25 years of experience and has become a sought-out expert on advocacy and policy development, diversity and inclusion, economic development, business development and organizational strategic planning and management. One of Towanda's colleagues stated, "the breadth and depth of her experience, in particular, with advocacy, strategic planning and implementation of sustainable economic development, business development, diversity, inclusion and equity programs has been extremely valuable to our organization and those stakeholders fortune enough to procure her services."

Towanda is a highly skilled and accredited international "Activational" life and business coach/consultant, motivational and business public speaker, author, rainmaker and trusted business mentor. She has journeyed through progressive years climbing the proverbial "corporate ladder" that remains a persistent challenge for women of color.

Towanda leveraged this challenge when she realized there is more power and influence in constructing your own ladder through her mindset and actions that have served to help women (and men) of color ascend the ranks in corporate, government and entrepreneurship.

HOW I SLAYED HER
TOWANDA LIVINGSTON

I woke up strapped to the hospital bed not knowing where I was and how I got there? I mean, I knew where I was, in the hospital and I knew I tried to kill myself, but how did I get here? In this horrible moment in time, I was just 15 years old and ready to give up on life. I was surrounded by white coat wearing white doctors and nurses (who by their eyes had judged me as another statistic), my grandmother and mother; I was crying out to Mommy and Momma to make the doctors stop, to help me. The room smelled of vomit, stank of hopelessness, and the doctors were shoving a huge clear hose down my nose to pump my stomach. I was gagging and thought I would choke to death as they pumped water down the hose and drew it back out until all the pills were recovered. See, I had swallowed a few bottles of my grandmother's prescription pills; the doctors and nurses were trying to save my life. A life I was ready to carelessly throw away. The "Her" was back again; and the "Her" brought her minions with her. Her minions were self-hate, self-doubt, self-sabotage, guilt, shame and defeat. Oh, yeah, "Her" came to play and to win.

The whiteness of the light bouncing on the stark white coats of the doctors blinded me and put me in an intentional daze; however, I could see the look on my mother and grandmother's faces. Shit, I can still see their faces. It was a look that was mixed with fear, disappointment and embarrassment; I felt as though I had broken their hearts and that made me want to die even more. I needed to escape this relentless pain. I rationalized; they would be better off without me; I was so sure of that. The smell of tar had broken my daze; they were force feeding me a tar drink and other fluids to help combat the potential poisoning of the pills; they didn't know I was already poisoned by my own self-hate, self-sabotage, depression, guilt, shame and selfishness. I tried to kill myself because my boyfriend at the time rejected me. As I reflect on that moment, I realize, that the very things that were tormenting me, I invited in—not only did I invite them in, I allowed them to come in and set up shop in my head and heart. When I was younger, I was told I was too black, too fat and too ugly for someone to love me. I was told that I would probably have to get a family member to take me to my proms or dances. As a child, I rejected these labels and assumptions, or at least I thought I did; I put on an "impenetrable veil" of confidence, courage and self-love, or at least I thought I did. As a child, I did not know that poisonous seeds were being planted in my mind and that I would cultivate and help grow into "Her."

Wow, I am now 50 years-old, and as I reflect on that moment in the hospital, I am grateful that God stepped in and saved my life. I can remember the first time I tried to kill myself, I was in eighth grade. I had gone into the bathroom and consumed a huge jar of medicinal cream and one of the students told my teacher, Mr. Sindecki. Mr. Sindecki, he was not only handsome, he was an awesome and compassionate teacher; and on this day, he became a divine intervention. Isn't it amazing how God will use inconspicuous people to fulfill his purpose? The stunned look on Mr. Sindecki's face said it all, he could not believe I had tried to kill myself. I shared with Mr. Sindecki that I was tired of being fat, ugly and dark-skinned and I wanted to be like the other students in my class, pretty, light-skinned and poplar. I wanted to be pretty, fair-skinned and loveable like my mother. I shared, I did not want to live the rest of my life as this black, fat and ugly girl. Mr. Sindecki was stunned to say the least; however, what he shared with me that day saved my life and I will never forget what he said. "Towanda, don't you know how special you are? Most of the kids in that class will never achieve what you are destined to achieve in your life. Towanda your beauty will come, and you have something more precious than popularity; you have greatness inside of you! Popularity is like a fad and it will wane; however, greatness will give you influence and courage to change the world. Trust me, it lasts longer than popularity. Towanda, you have been marked with greatness and you have so much more to give the world. So, giving up now is not an option and not the answer. I promise you Towanda, tomorrow things will look so very different. Please do not ever try to hurt yourself again; there is a whole world waiting for you and trust me the world needs you." Mr. Sindecki promised me he would not tell my mom about the incident, only if I promised to come to him if I ever felt that way again. I promised. By the time I was 19 years old I would have tried to kill myself over five times by various means. "Her" was winning! I knew I had to slay her if I wanted to truly live the life God promised me and walk into my God-ordained purpose. My famous saying is *"Either by inspiration or desperation you will be pushed into your purpose"* and I developed this saying for dark times such as these, and "HER" was pushing me hard!

It is my belief that a woman is always in a state of becoming the best version of herself; and she will have to slay many versions of her past selves ("HER") as she evolves. There is a constant struggle within every woman between who she use-to-be and who she is destined to become. In order to counterattack, persevere and conqueror, she must have access to divine resources, grace, faith and a powerful support system, such as, but not limited to: God-fearing women; faithful and confident women; women who have made winning a habit; women who have made it through the painful process of transformation and loss; women who have amassed an arsenal of divine stratagems to navigate the "high waters" of life, love and career; and women who have surrendered to their limitless possibilities. To defeat "Her" a woman will need to chase the things that scare her the most. She will need to chase her lions, wolves and bears by running towards these fears and being prepared to slay them. It is either her or them; and from what I know about being a woman, those bears, lions and wolves better run.

So, how did I slay "HER?" She was slain with prayer, faith, steadfast determination, divine purpose, surrounding myself with sista-friends who lived on purpose, the strength and prayers of my mother and grandmother and of course lots of therapy. *It is okay to need Jesus and a therapist.* As I slayed "Her" and her minions, I became more self-aware, self-confident and determined to succeed. Before you start to applaud me, I must share that it was these things that saved me that would lead me on another journey of self-discovery and into battle with the next "HER." I was in a transition phase (a planting season) and I had to leave family, friends, bad habits, addictions, proclivities that undermined my dreams and purpose behind. This was the hardest part of the planting season. I had to leave folks that I love behind and the behaviors that fed those relationships. I was devastated, I was conflicted and the "Her" name guilt and shame was making an encore. *Did I tell you that "HER" will reappear in your life if you let her in?* "Her" is just like getting sick with the flu; you take antibiotics, get well and the next strand is stronger, so you must take more potent antibiotics. Prayer acts as the immunization shot for "Her," the stronger the "Her" the more powerful and purposeful the prayers. That is "Her" and her minions, they love chaos and mass distractions; in fact, they thrive on them. *Damn, these bitches won't die!* It's like self-hate, self-doubt, depression, guilt and shame are on the bench waiting to get back on the playing field again; and they have been working out, so they are stronger, sneakier and deadlier. That is why you must have unyielding faith, pray without ceasing, keep a strong circle of influence and have powerful intercessors. Between the ages of 15 and 21, I would experience great losses and wins. You see, I was in constant battles for what was earmarked by God for me. I would not come out of these battles without permanent scars, wounds and consequences. I had changed, my views had changed, my dreams had changed, how I walked and talked had changed.

The battles continued. Between the ages of 15 and 21 I had five abortions, and being Catholic, I knew I was going *to hell with gasoline drawers on,* for sure. "Her" was back on attack. At age 15, I had more body than brains, and I was discretely promiscuous, or at least that is what I told myself to help me sleep at night and to help me face myself in the mirror. I had the disease to please, and was determined to find love, a love I did not have for myself. I was not going to fail. I was not going to be a statistic. I was going to make it, damn it! My mother had me when she was 16 years old and that changed the course of her life forever, and she did not want me to suffer the same fate. "Her" shows up in generational curses. I was not going to let my mommy down; I was going to make her proud and break the bondage of these damn generational curses.

The boys and men I found myself attracted to were just as broken as I was and really did not want to be with me (or deserve me), but I was no quitter, I was going to make them love me. So, I tried to buy them, I gave them my body and unknowingly I gave them a piece of my soul. The first time I got pregnant, at age 16, my mother knew before me, because she was keeping track of my menstrual cycle. I was naïve and sure I was not pregnant. My mom and I went to the doctors, and sure enough I was pregnant. I cannot explain the disappointment on my mother's face. It was if someone shot her in her heart or delivered her a gut punch that she could not catch her breath from. "Her" the generational curse had caught up to me. The look of disappointment on my mother's face that day, was not just about the pregnancy, it was the feeling of loss—loss of the dreams and hopes she had for my life and that I had for my life. She felt those dreams, possibilities and hope slipping away from me and that broke her heart.

I was shocked. Looking back, I don't know why I was shocked, I was having unprotected sex with my long-term boyfriend. I was overcome with guilt and shame. At the time I was attending an all-girls Catholic High School and although there were many girls that were pregnant, we did not discuss it and we did not discuss contraception in school. Premarital sex and contraception were sins and were not discussed in Catholic School. So, not only was I consumed by shame and guilt at home, I was flooded with shame and guilt at school. Ms. Oberholzer, my chemistry teacher was more than a teacher to me. I adored her and I believe she adored me as well. I shared with Ms. Oberholzer the predicament I found myself in and although I could see the disappointment on her face, she was compassionate and tender with me. What Ms. Oberholzer said to me that day, I carry with me daily. God's divine intervention shows up and shows out again. "Her" was not going to win! Ms. Oberholzer stated, "Towanda, forgive yourself because God already has. What is done is done and either it has come to bless you or teach you a lesson; listen with your heart and mind and God will reveal to you his purpose. Towanda, I know you have a tough choice ahead of you and know that whatever you decide, I will be here for you. You have a very bright future; I know you are destined for greatness. Towanda, I need you to believe that you have a purpose. As a woman you will have to make some difficult choices in life that will come with some stiff consequences—Towanda, you can weather any storm that comes your way, just lean into God, trust God and he will show up in amazing ways." Needless to say, Ms. Oberholzer was my favorite teacher in high school.

Ms. Oberholzer was right, I had to make a tough decision, do I keep my baby, or do I have an abortion. Let me just say, I have always been and will always be pro-choice. The choice I was about to make, (my mother left the choice up to me), would change the trajectory of my life forever. My boyfriend wanted me to have an abortion and I felt like my family wanted me to have an abortion, but the decision carried with it so much weight that it almost broke me into pieces. So, I had an abortion. Having an abortion freed me from my right to become a mother, but it also enslaved me. I would be shackled to guilt, shame and depression due to the five abortions I would have from ages 15 to 21. *Life has showed me time and time again that choices comes with consequences, so, choose wisely and don't bet with what you are not willing to lose.* From the ages of 15 to 21, I had used the convenience of abortions as contraception without fully understanding the long-term consequences that I would soon have to face at the age of 30.

On June 25, 1999, my husband and I welcomed our premature baby girl into the world, Bryce Alexis Livingston. On June 29, 1999, the worst day of our lives, my husband and I lost our baby girl. I have had doctors tell me that the five abortions had no impact on this horrible outcome. However, I believe differently, my careless choices earlier in life had led to my child's death. I blamed myself for the hurt I caused my husband and the hopeful grandparents. I will go on to have five miscarriages after the loss of our daughter. I considered myself a failure. As a woman, I failed because I could not do what was natural for women, give life to a healthy baby. I denied my loving husband, my parents and my mother-in-law children and grandchildren all because I was reckless as a teenager and young woman. "Her" does not play fair; she was sent to destroy me and deliver me to Satan. The weight of guilt, shame and depression that I felt allowed the other

"Hers," that I thought I slayed in and it became so overwhelming. I am ashamed to say I hated God when Bryce died. Also, I am ashamed to admit that although my mother would give birth to a major source of my inspiration, my little sister (my "potato), when I was 17 years old, I was jealous of my mother. I was mad at my mother because I was having these abortions to keep from bringing a baby home and here she was having a baby. My mother did not know about three of my five abortions, but I found myself blaming her. Do you see a common theme? I was blaming God and everyone else for the decisions I made, for the death of my baby and for the babies my husband and I would never get to raise and dream with and for. I even blamed by boyfriend when I had my first abortion, I would say "only if he loved me enough" or "only if I was more loveable," we could have had our baby. "Her" loves for you to look backwards, she loves when you dwell in the would-haves, should-haves and could-haves. That is why to this day I do not believe in watering dead plants. Let the dead bury the dead and I was not dead yet.

So, how did I slay her? Whew, she was a goliath! She was slain with more ferocious faith, potent prayer, divine purpose, a loving husband, a ride and live sister, a beautiful niece, surrounding myself with a tougher than steel sistah squad and pourers (*pourers are folks that pour their faith, knowledge, wisdom, skills and abilities into you.*) who refused to give up on me and the unyielding strength and prayers of my mother, grandmother and prior generations--and of course lots of therapy.

It took a 50-year journey to learn and apply hard-won wisdom. However, what 50 years has taught me is that my journey was never about me, it was ALL about God. When I was younger, I was always ambitious and a giver for the wrong reasons. However, between the ages of 22 and 25, I woke up, something shifted in me, and I became a selfless go-getter and go-giver. It became more important for me to serve more, do more, love more, forgive more and give more. I wanted to see and help others thrive and fulfill their God-given purposes. Instead of focusing on climbing the corporate ladder and making money; I became a ladder builder and a rainmaker for professionals and diverse entrepreneurs. Every day I wake up with purpose that moves from my head, to my heart to my hands and this is how I continue to slay "Her." Believe it or not, you can slay your "Hers" too; if and only if you are willing to be vulnerable, ask for help, do the spade work and grab on and hold on to your faith in God. Trust me, my 50 years on this side of heaven has shown one undeniable fact—if you do your part, GOD will show up in a nick-of-time to do his part.

Martha Cooper-Hudson

Martha Cooper-Hudson is a woman of greatness on a mission to help others realize their greatness within. She has been called to equip, inspire, motivate and empower women to live a life of health and wealth while they stand up, suit up and walk in their purpose. For over 10 years,

Martha's message has been and will continue to be: *"When you have a dream, goal, purpose and a will to succeed no matter the cost, time doesn't matter."*

Martha built a multi-million dollar organization during her career in network marketing and became a highly sought after motivational speaker and trainer to individuals and companies around the United States. Her belief in hard work and dedication allowed her to start two highly profitable companies that have benefited the lives of hundreds of thousands of people.

The multi-talented businesswoman and author is rapidly emerging as one of the most dynamic life coaches and empowerment leaders.

JOURNEY TO 50
MARTHA COOPER-HUDSON

Wow, what can I say about my road and journey to 50! I can definitely say that it wasn't an easy journey but it was a necessary journey to get me to this point. Let's go back to year 36 and move forward.

In the words of the famous poet Langston Hughes *"life for me ain't been no crystal stair"*. My journey to 50 was filled with a lot of discomfort, potholes, distractions, setbacks, great losses, health scares, cloudiness, and uncertainty. But through it all, I learned more than ever how strong I was, how resilient I was, and how determined I was to not allow Satan to take my life, my hope, and or my faith.

Once you have discovered and or realized your purpose on earth, not only does Satan get mad as hell, but he goes into overdrive to delay, derail, and or abort what God has placed in you. Knowing that your purpose in life is bigger than you, and that it's not about you, allows you to take the hits and the setbacks in order for you to reach the very people that need what God has given you to birth on this planet.

Fourteen (14) years ago our lives changed forever, and I faced the hardest obstacle that I've ever faced in my life. I found myself fighting for my family, as my husband fought for his life. At the age of 40 my husband was diagnosed with Stage 3A colorectal cancer. A diagnosis that we never saw coming. There were no signs and or symptoms until that very day, which left me with no time to prepare for what we were going to face. Did I mention that we had a one year old, a three-year-old, a mortgage that was $3800 at the time, and a letter from my husband's job stating that they were downsizing his department (yeah right).

Can I be real with you? I was scared as hell and didn't know what I was going to do, but I knew I had to do something. I knew at that very moment failure was not an option and quitting didn't exist. Between the tears, me questioning God, and having a very sick husband, God spoke to me and said "my daughter you have everything that you need within you to get out of this situation." Keep your eyes on me, your ears to my lips, and your hands on the plow and everything will be alright.

At that moment of me saying yes to his will, a shift happened within me and I learned just how powerful the word YES would become in my life.

Ask yourself have you ever : 1.) Dimmed your light for someone else to feel adequate in your presence. 2.) Are you going to a job that no longer feed you, serve you, or pay you your worth. 3.) Are you existing versus living 4.) Are you waiting on validation from the very people that do not celebrate you but tolerate you? 5.) Are your dreams and goals eating at you but you do not know how to let them out. 6.) Are you Ready to live your BEST LIFE?

I said and did all of those things to myself over the past 14 years. But I stand here today as a Prime Time Woman who never gave up and who RediscovHERd everything about me. The good, the bad, and the ugly!

During this very critical time a transformation happened within me. I felt as if God placed me in a cocoon to go threw the metamorphosis stage, in order for me to emerge as this beautiful, strong, highly driven and determined, butterfly that will never dim her light, mute her voice, or settle for anything less than what GOD has for me.

At that moment I said "YES" to:

- waking up my dreams and goals

- never being in that situation again and allowing a job to have that much power over our life
- living my best life
- building a business empire that would have not one but seven strong streams of income
- Six figures at all times in my bank account
- knowing my value and stop allowing others to coupon and or discount my skills
- helping every highly driven women on a mission to stand up, suit up and boss up unapologetically
- chasing my purpose and not the paper.

During this time in my life the Extractor of Purpose was born, the Comeback Coach emerged and life for me became a crystal stair. I found out that I was built Ford tough and that no matter what came my way, I could handle it because my God would always be bigger than my problems. Due to my hard work, dedication, and my willingness to win, I was able to create an empire that no man could take away from me and my family ever again. An Empire that was built on a solid foundation with God as my CEO and a team that not only saw the vision, but also made the vision their own.

My purpose on this planet became clearer and clearer and I accepted the assignment that God had chosen for me to do.

That purpose and mission was to equip, inspire, motivate, and empower, highly driven women on a mission and a few good men to stand up, suit up, and boss up in their purpose. On that realization RediscovHER and Boss'd up Business Academy was born.

A wise and very wealthy man whom I'm proud to call my mentor once said to me, " Martha, if you show and help people get the things that they desire, and show them how to accomplish their goals, they will always help you succeed. He said to me, if you keep your motives pure, and not about you, you will never have to look for a dime ever again. I took that to heart, stamped it on my memory bank, and from that day forward, I've never had to chase a dollar, because when my dreams collided with my purpose money ran me over.

On the day of my 45th birthday ReDiscover her the company was born. A couple of years later bossed up Business Academy was created. That birthday started my five-year journey to my 50th which made me more determined to impact as many women's lives as I possibly could. Creating systems & programmes that allowed me to teach, share, and show women that their dreams, their goals, and their missions, doesn't have to change or be put on the back burner because their last name changed, their titles changed, and or their positions on their jobs changed. I have been able to do just that through my conferences, webinars, workshops, speaking engagements, and my Me, Myself, and I women's weekend getaways.

After overcoming many obstacles in life, accomplishing all of my goals, and reaching the level of success that most people only dream about, here comes life again! Damn, Damn, Damn! Are you serious? God why me? Why now? Just when I thought this setback was the trick of the enemy, it was actually a blessing from above. In order for me to go to the next level God had to eliminate some people that were not appointed by him but attached by themselves. That hurt a lot because I thought they would be in my life forever. The elevator door opened and they had to exit. That very moment made me realize that everyone can not go where you are going. everyone cannot handle the air at the aptitude that God is taking you. Be okay with that, because it's for your own good and the birth of your purpose.

On December 5th 2018, I made a decision that I would take control of my health and be in the best physical shape of my life by the time I turned 50. I told my husband and my children what I wanted to do and they all laughed at me. Now let me say, that they had good cause to laugh, because to know me is to know that I despised going to the gym. There was nothing sexy about that at all. I knew that my decision was going to take true dedication, commitment, and hard work to accomplish this goal. That night I went live on Facebook to share with my tribe what I had decided to do. I needed the accountability and they kept my feet to the fire for 365 days.

During my physical transformation God was also doing a mindset transformation as he conducted a RESET within me. I like to call it the SHIFT! Which made me realize my greatest strengths, allowed me to have some of my greatest successes as he molded me into that fine piece of china, and the highest quality of purpose, as I evolved into that Prime Time Woman. A woman who is classy and sassy. A woman who will no longer have her voice silenced, her dreams hidden, and being the best kept secret because I am boldly entering into the Prime of my life and I am doing so unapologetically!

No more games...I am living life to the fullest on my terms while I OWN MY POWER! To my amazing sisters reading this book. I challenge you to start discovering who you really are? To start loving all of you? To know what makes you happy and not settle just because. Be ok with saying NO and know that you are MORE than ENOUGH. Your value can never be measured because you are a priceless gem, so stop allowing others to coupon your gifts and talents for the sake of building their dreams.

But as you continue on this journey called life always remember if you light another sister's candle yours will never go out and if you light enough people's candle they will start to say "What a beautiful wildfire that is."

Remember to Support, Strengthen, and LIft HER up as you make room at the table because someone behind you is watching.

Dr. Sharon H. Porter

Dr. Sharon H. Porter (Dr. Sharon) resides in the Washington, DC area. She is the Owner of SHP Enterprise, the umbrella entity of **Perfect Time SHP LLC, G.R.I.N.D. Entrepreneur Network, Write the Book Now!, and SHP Media and Broadcasting**. She is the host of the I Am Dr. Sharon Show and CoFounder and Owner of Vision & Purpose (V&P) Magazine. Dr. Sharon is Executive Director of the Next in Line to Lead Aspiring Principal Academy.

Dr. Sharon is the author of *The Power of Networking: How to Achieve Success With Business Networking, Next In Line to Lead: The Voice of the Assistant Principal , Class of 2017 What's Next?"* the *Women Who Lead Book Series, The HBCU Experience Anthology book series,* and *North Carolina Girls Living In a Maryland World*

Dr. Sharon has served as an educator for over 25 years, serving in the roles of classroom teacher, Curriculum Coordinator, Instructional Specialist, Test Development Specialist, assistant principal, Leadership Development Coach, and elementary and middle school principal.

She is a graduate of Howard University, Walden University, Johns Hopkins University, Nationa-lLouis University and Winston-Salem State University. Dr. Sharon holds a National Association of Elementary School Principal Mentor Certification and is a Certified Gallup-Strengths Coach.

She is a proud member of Delta Sigma Theta Sorority, Incorporated, International Association of Women (IAW), and an Official Member of the Forbes Coaches Council, Professional Women of Winston-Salem.

Connect with Dr. Sharon at shpenterprise.com

PHENOMENALLY 50

DR. SHARON H. PORTER

Saturday, September 27, 1969 Sharon Denese Hargro came into this world. I could have never imagined all that life had to offer in the years and decades to come. I have learned so much in these 50 years. I have experienced joy, pain, disappointment, fear, and grief just to name a few.

Friday, September 27, 2019 I was blessed to turn 50 years old. FIFTY… The BIG 5…0… I can recall growing up thinking 50 was "old", like "Grandma" old… As one of my former pastors always would say "just keep on living"… It is true… Any negative thoughts you have about various situations, if you live long enough, you will see through different lenses.

I truly feel that I am living my best life right at this moment. I have learned so much about life, myself, and people in general. Truly, "if only I knew then what I know now," my life would perhaps be a different, but I believe that everything happens as it should. The goal is to receive the blessing and learn the lesson.

I grew up in Winston-Salem, NC and for many years I didn't really think beyond the state of North Carolina. My childhood was happy and innocent. I was surrounded by family and spent a great deal of time with my girl cousins. We did everything together.

Sometimes things don't work out as you plan. In high school, I had my sights on attending college in Charlotte. That didn't happen and I ended up staying in my hometown attending Winston-Salem State University (WSSU). I didn't know it at the time, but it was the best decision I could have made. I had an amazing college experience. My most rewarding experience other than graduating was pledging Delta Sigma Theta Sorority, Inc. I was initiated into the sorority on April 10, 1990 in the Gamma Phi Chapter. The sisterhood that was formed close to 30 years ago is still going strong.

You must experience new things. After graduating from WSSU I began teaching in Charlotte. I was determined to live in the Queen City. After about three or four years, I desired to experience another part of the country. I ended up in the Washington, DC area. While I had visited the area often, I never thought I would call the area home. Moving to the DC area gave me a new sense of purpose. I was amazed at the diversity and the opportunities I was afforded. I would go on to earn several degrees and get a few promotions within the school district. I was experiencing great success. I was appointed as an assistant principal in 2001was married in 2002 and I started a doctoral program in 2006. things were really moving. I had completed two years of my doctoral program which consisted of all of the required coursework. Year three was the dissertation. I would later serve in several central office positions and then ultimately I became a principal.

Leadership would play an important part in my career trajectory. My doctoral research was based on leadership development and principal preparation. This focus would extend beyond my career. I built my entire business around developing others. In 2019, I was fortunate to open the Next In Line to Lead Aspiring Principal Leadership Academy (APLA).

The year 2019 was a healing year for me. I went through a lot in 2018 personally as well as professionally. I was determined to make 2019 Phenomenal! One thing that became clear to me was you cannot continue to operate business as usual. I had to find new circles, new events to attend, just a new perspective on life. I refused to continue doing the same things I'd done in the past. I had to experience new things.

Spend time with the ones you love. October 2008, I was left feeling numb and lost. An emptiness was felt after losing my father. He had been sick for several years. Even before I got married in 2002. He was unable to attend my wedding due to his illness. I would go home occasionally. I found myself with so much to do that I didn't always take the time to travel to North Carolina. I have few regrets in life and that is certainly one of them. I wished I had taken the time to go home for every occasion. I saw my dad alive for the last time on my birthday in 2008. Five days later he was gone. He was such a great dad. I am a lot like him. You have to take and make the time to spend with those you love. Truly tomorrow is not promised. The loss of two of my first cousins in 2018 gave me a jolt I had never experienced before. I was truly grateful to see my 50th birthday.

Keep Grinding. I didn't finish that doctoral degree during my first program. I just couldn't regain my focus after the death of my father. I relocated back to North Carolina for almost three years. When I returned to Maryland I had the opportunity to begin another doctoral program at Howard

University. I started that program in 2014 and I was able to complete it in 2017. When you set a goal, you keep grinding until it is reached.

Keep Grinding has been my motto, my mantra. I oftentimes have to whisper it to myself. There are so many things I want to pursue and accomplish. It's not always easy. I've learned to silence the noise and "keep grinding". I often say, no matter who, no matter what, you must keep grinding. Keep grinding for me simply means don't stop, don't quit, keep it moving!

Live your dreams. It was as if I had a rebirth after earning my doctoral degree. I begin to write and publish books, I became the host of my own interview show and started a coaching and consulting firm. I decided it was time to wake up and live my dreams. So many people only dream of doing things, but never put the action behind it to make it a reality. It is time-out for wishing and hoping. It's ok to dream, but at some point, you must wake up and live the dream!

I am the co-owner of Vision & Purpose (V&P)LifeStyle Magazine. This is something I often thought about doing. It was not until my now, business partner shared that she wanted to own a magazine that I truly acted on the idea. I had been playing around with some designs and would create different publications for my podcasts and businesses. When you surround yourself with the right people, there should be evidence of growth.

I challenge women everywhere, younger, older, all women to live your dreams. When something has been placed on your heart or in your mind, do it! One of my former spiritual leaders would always so, "Life Can Be Beautiful"... It most certainly can. It doesn't mean it will be easy... It is hard work, but so worth it. Live Your Dreams!

I am indeed grateful to God for allowing me to see my 50th birthday in 2019. There was a time I would not make a big deal about my birthday. After losing six family members in 2018, my perspective changed. I am not only 50, but I am Phenomenally 50 and will celebrate each day as the blessing it is.

www.ingramcontent.com/pod-product-compliance
Lightning Source LLC
Chambersburg PA
CBHW030235170426
43201CB00006B/231